TORQUAY

of Yesteryear

Leslie Retallick

GH00691825

OBELISK PUBLICATIONS

ALSO BY THE AUTHOR
Pictorial Torquay

OTHER OBELISK PUBLICATIONS ABOUT THIS AREA

Torquay, *Chips Barber* • Paignton, *Chips Barber* • Brixham, *Chips Barber*
Torbay in Colour – Torquay Paignton Brixham, *Chips Barber*
Around and About the Haldon Hills – Revisited, *Chips Barber*
Pub Walks in and around the Haldon Hills, *Brian Carter*
Nine Short Pub Walks in and around Torquay, *Brian Carter*
Torquay United – The First 70 Years, *Laura Joint*
Pictures of Paignton, Parts I, II and III, *Peter Tully*
Cockington, *Jo Connell* • Colourful Cockington, *Chips Barber*
Brixham of Yesteryear, Parts I, II and III, *Chips Barber*
From Brixham… With Love, *Chips Barber*
The Ghosts of Brixham, *Graham Wyley*
The Ghosts of Berry Pomeroy Castle, *Deryck Seymour*
The Great Little Totnes Book, *Chips Barber* • The Ghosts of Totnes, *Bob Mann*
Newton Abbot in the News, *Brian Thomas*
Newton Abbot Album, Parts I and II, *Fred Tozer*
Murders and Mysteries in Devon, *Ann James*
Made in Devon, *Chips Barber and David FitzGerald*
Place-names in Devon, *Chips Barber*
We have over 180 Devon-based titles; for a list of current books please send SAE to
2 Church Hill, Pinhoe, Exeter, EX4 9ER or telephone (01392) 468556

Acknowledgements:
Photographs on pages 15 (bottom), 16, 20 (bottom) and 30 from the Torre Abbey Collection.
Page 8 (bottom) belongs to Chips Barber.
Sources:
Arthur Ellis, *An Historical Survey of Torquay*; John Pike, *Torquay, The Place and the People*;
Peter Gray (for information on photo on page 32 (bottom); *Herald Express*;
Torquay Reference Library; Fisher Barham, *Torbay Transport*.

This book is dedicated to my godson, Michael Hardie

"Every Morn and every Night
Some are born to Sweet Delight"
William Blake, *Auguries of Innocence*

First published in 2002 by
Obelisk Publications, 2 Church Hill, Pinhoe, Exeter, Devon
Designed and Typeset by Sally Barber
Printed in Great Britain
by Colour C Ltd, Tiverton, Devon

TORQUAY
of Yesteryear

Most books of views of Torquay tend to start at the harbour, which is fair enough – it is, after all, the place from where the town got its name. The view from Waldon Hill has always been a popular one for postcard makers. This is quite an early one; the Mallock Memorial (or the Clock Tower as most people know it) is missing, so the view must date from before 1902, when work on the tower began. The publisher must have decided that it was a terribly dull picture, as he had an artist draw in the figures in the foreground.

Below is a view from Vane Hill, of the harbour in about 1905. Behind the coal stores on North Quay stretch the Princess Gardens, laid out in 1894 on land reclaimed from the sea; they are named after Princess Louise, daughter of Queen Victoria.

Built in 1899, the SS *Pioneer* was sold to William Mellor of Torquay in 1906. With her sister ship the *King Edward*, which is just visible moored behind the *Pioneer*, she provided a regular ferry service to Brixham and Paignton, as well as longer trips along the coast to Teignmouth and round to Dartmouth.

It's often overlooked that Torquay harbour was built primarily for trade, and it was only in fairly recent years that cargo ships have been replaced by pleasure boats. The two scenes below show a vessel unloading timber from Scandinavia in August 1936.

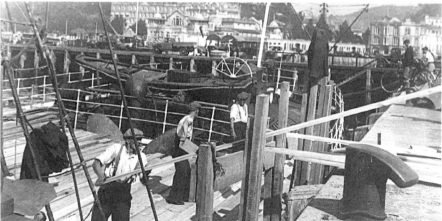

4

Here we see the outer harbour in the the 1950s, with a magnificent three-master tied up at the harbour wall, and an almost equally fine private steam yacht moored in the centre.

"When Mother said you were a good catch dear, I don't think this is what she had in mind!" could have been the caption for this postcard of folk fishing off Haldon Pier in about 1900.

Below we see Cary Parade in the 1890s, when it was a row of charming and genteel cottages. Only faint traces remain of the old cottages today, and you've got to look jolly hard to find them behind the slot-machine arcade that now occupies the site!

Three extinct hotels can be seen in this view of Abbey Place in 1900: the Cary Hotel (on the extreme left), the London Hotel (on the right) and the Central Hotel (unsurprisingly, in the centre). Also in the shot is Addisons Dairy, whose tearooms later became the place for an afternoon cuppa.

Vintage car enthusiasts would love to get their hands on the gleaming limousines lined up on the Strand in this scene from the mid-1920s. In spite of the number of cars and trams about, the pedestrians obviously felt it was perfectly safe to wander about in the middle of the road. I wouldn't recommend it today!

This is the Strand in 1904. The Mallock Memorial, completed the previous year, stands in pristine splendour. It was built as a memorial to Richard Mallock of Cockington Court, one-time MP for Torquay.

"No, I said turn right, not left" could be the excuse for this slight parking problem on Victoria Parade in the 1930s!

Above is Victoria Parade in 1908. The Sailors' Rest, in the centre of the photograph, had been opened by Agnes Weston five years earlier to join those already established in Plymouth and Portsmouth. Note the cannon in the foreground being used as a bollard.

Below are Beacon Cove and the much loved (and much missed) Marine Spa, in the 1950s. Beacon Cove was always regarded as the locals' beach, and its closure, when the seriously unloved Coral Island replaced the Marine Spa, was (and still is) a source of rancour locally.

(Opposite, top) The landward end of Princess Pier once sported this diving stage, which came into its own at the Torquay Regatta each year, when the boards, seen on the right of the stage, were used for the diving events. I'm not at all sure that I'd fancy diving into the somewhat murky waters of the outer harbour these days.

(Middle) The diving stage hadn't been built when this shot of the 1901 regatta was taken. The area used for the swimming and diving events can be seen in the near corner of the outer harbour, with a large crowd assembled to watch the goings-on.

(Bottom) The Rock Walk, or more correctly The Royal Terrace Gardens, opened in 1893. This view, taken shortly after the opening, shows the collecting box for the Torquay Lifeboat, then still stationed at Beacon Quay. It also shows a positively splendid pram.

Torquay of Yesteryear

Rock Walk, Torquay.   2358.

Here we have the seafront in the late 1930s, showing the newly widened and laid-out promenade. The area between Torquay Harbour and Abbey Sands has all been reclaimed from the sea over the years, the final (so far!) widening being carried out between 1934 and 1935.

Below we can see Abbey Sands and the seafront from the Rock Walk. Note an early form of Crazy Golf laid out in the grass in Abbey Park.

This picture dates from about 1900, or maybe even a few years earlier, when horse-drawn transport still reigned supreme. I know that horse manure was said to be good for the roses, but it must have made crossing the street a bit difficult, especially in the full-length skirts and dresses that ladies wore in those days.

Although demolished only a few years ago, the row of arches built as a bathing platform in the early 1930s at one end of Abbey Sands is already a fading memory. Notice how everyone in the picture is muffled up with thick coats and hats – it must have been August!

Ever since Abbey Park opened to the public in late 1924, the flower bed at the Belgrave Road entrance has been used for an annual display, usually a commemorative coat of arms. This superb example was created in honour of the coronation of King George VI in 1937.

In the scene below it is the summer of 1911, and a Paignton-bound tram has stopped near the Grand Hotel to pick up passengers. The tramway system had just been converted to an overhead power supply, as the original supply, laid between the tracks, was found to be time-consuming and expensive to maintain. It was also dangerous: anyone stepping between the tracks at the wrong moment was likely to receive an electrifying experience – literally!

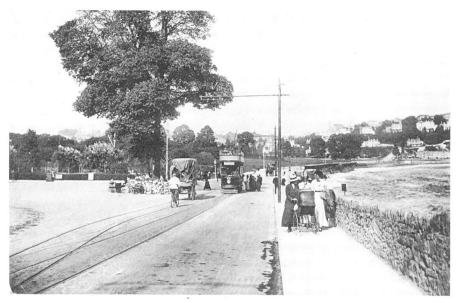

This is Corbyn Sands in the late 1930s. The dark spectre of the Second World War was starting to cast a shadow on people's lives, but you'd never know it from this sunny scene. Drawn up on the beach is what I at first took to be a very large model yacht, but is actually a very small real one. Perhaps one of the seven dwarves was down on holiday!

Below is another late 1930s view, but these really are model yachts, on the pond in King's Gardens. The original council minutes state that the pond was built for the use of 'juvenile yachtsmen'.

To celebrate the Silver Jubilee of King George V and Queen Mary in 1935, a pageant with parades and traditional dancing was held on the Recreation Ground, with all the local schools taking part.

Snow, although not unknown in South Devon, is still a rare enough event to send local photographers into a complete frenzy of picture taking. This is the King's Drive on 7 February 1955, when it still had an avenue of trees.

In 1898, after the death of his elder brother Robert, Colonel Lucius Cary inherited Torre Abbey, but was unable to live there as it was occupied by Robert's widow. She died in 1907, and in July of that year there was a gathering of the great and the good at the Abbey to welcome the Colonel and his wife home.

From 1949 to 1959, the Torquay Open Air Theatre operated in the grounds of Torre Abbey, in front of the Spanish Barn. Over forty productions were mounted during this period, and this view, from the roof of the Mohun Gatehouse, was taken during a performance of *Lost in the Stars*, in July 1955. The 'blacking up' of several members of the all-white cast would be severely frowned on today.

Apart from the performances put on by local and visiting amateur dramatic societies, the Open Air Theatre also attracted touring professional companies, including the BBC's Ariel Players. In 1959 they staged a performance of *Charley's Aunt*, with a youthful Richard Baker in the title role.

Another venue for theatricals was the Pavilion, opened in 1912. Over the years it's been put to a number of purposes including a theatre, a skating rink and, currently, a shopping centre. Its original function was, however, as a concert hall, some of the greatest names in the world of British music performing there. Torquay also once boasted its own municipal orchestra, and this shot shows them in full flight at the Pavilion in the 1930s. The orchestra was disbanded in 1953.

Looking down Fleet Street towards the harbour, the tram tracks are in evidence, but not the overhead wires, so this view must be about 1910.

Town Hall, Torquay.

The Italianate tower of the old town hall, seen on the left of this 1903 view, still stands, but most of the buildings on the right hand side of the picture were demolished when the large roundabout by the Post Office was made. The gentleman on the extreme right is no doubt wondering what the photographer is up to.

One of my personal favourites is this view of Union Street in about 1900. There's such a lot going on in the picture, from the variety of traffic in the street to the various people milling around, such as the lady with the parasol on the left, and the man standing completely unconcerned in the middle of the road. The portico on the right belongs to the Union Hotel, long since demolished. The chap with his arms folded, standing next to the cart in the centre of the picture, looks as though he's delivering or collecting luggage for the hotel guests. He also looks as if he's going to do something nasty to the photographer if the latter doesn't go away soon!

Torquay of Yesteryear

We are now higher up Union Street, also in about 1900. Photographers were still a novelty, so the delivery boy to the left is risking a clip round the ear for dawdling by staring at the cameraman.

Below, it is five minutes to one on a day sometime between 1904 and 1911 (there's a tram in the background but no overhead wires). There's obviously great excitement about something, but what the occasion is, I haven't been able to find out.

Both World Wars had a great impact on the town. Not long after the start of the first one, a number of Belgian refugees arrived in Torquay. They were made welcome; this view shows them aboard two trams laid on to give them a tour of the town. An unexpected outcome of the arrival of the Belgians is that the young Agatha Miller (later Agatha Christie) used her memories of them to help create her detective Hercule Poirot.

Agatha Christie was a volunteer nurse during the First World War, working in the hospital set up in the Town Hall. This photograph shows the hospital, so the future 'Queen of the Whodunit' is no doubt somewhere among the staff lined up on the balcony.

In June 1915, nearly 300 wounded soldiers arrived in Torquay from Exeter, a fleet of cars being provided for them. They were taken to the Pavilion for entertainment and tea, after which they were given short trips around the bay on board the *King Edward*.

On to the Second World War, and Dad's Army is on the march! One of the local contingents of the Home Guard is pictured here, along Vaughan Parade.

(Opposite, top) As the Second World War gathered momentum, the Misses Madge and Kathleen Whitehead formed the Evacuated Mothers' Union Club in Torquay, to provide a centre for those who had been evacuated from other parts of the country. The club members, apart from providing mutual support, also busied themselves with helping the war effort in such ways as picking rose hips to make into syrup.

(Middle) Another task for the ladies of the Evacuated Mothers' Union Club was making camouflage netting.

(Bottom) A fair number of children were evacuated to Torquay during the war, and considerable efforts were made to make them feel welcome and to keep them entertained. This photograph shows some of the youngsters at a fancy dress competition held at Blythswood, in St Marychurch Road, in the summer of 1942.

(Above) The postmark on this card is 1949, but no doubt the picture was taken a few years earlier, probably when floodlighting was still a novelty following the blackout of the war years. Opened in the 1860s, the Imperial was one of the first purpose-built hotels in Torquay; it soon lived up to its name by attracting a fair smattering of British and continental royalty.

(Below) Bishopstowe, a large Victorian villa built in 1841 for the Bishop of Exeter, was converted into the Palace Hotel in 1921. This view was obviously taken shortly afterwards, with all the dancers having a 'jolly good time'.

(Opposite, top and middle) What were once three large Victorian villas in Chestnut Avenue, close to Torre Abbey, were later joined together to form the Rosetor and Roselea Hotels. They were graceful, elegant buildings, which were demolished to make way for the large lump of concrete known as the Riviera Centre. Why are most new buildings so ugly?

(Bottom) The Rosehill Children's Hospital, an early, and for that time very rare, example of a children's hospice, had been founded in 1888 in a small house in Babbacombe for children suffering from incurable diseases. In 1904, Mrs Louisa Cary gave the freehold of a plot of land in the Warberries to the Hospital Committee, in memory of her stepson Henry Cary, who had died during the Boer War; the new, larger hospital shown on this card was built on the site.

(Above) The view of Cockington in 1913 hasn't changed very much since; about the only real difference is that, to quote from Tolkien's *The Hobbit*, "there was less noise and more green".

(Below) One thing that has changed in Cockington is that the forge was at that time a genuine working one, and not just a tourist attraction. With horse power still a common sight on the local farms, the smith was no doubt kept fully occupied.

In the 1890s, the Torquay suburb of Chelston was growing so fast that the old parish church at Cockington could no longer cope with the numbers. A new church, St Matthew's, was built, and the first breaking of the ground was carried out by Miss C. Mallock of Cockington Court on 21 February 1895. Judging by the leafless state of the trees in the background, this picture may well record the event. The single villa in the background has since been joined by a large number of neighbours. Below, we see members of Torquay Leander Swimming and Lifesaving Club lined up at Peaked Tor Cove. The wording painted on the sign behind them would seem to indicate that a similar shot was taken each year for the club's annual Christmas Card.

(Opposite, top) Another group of (somewhat younger) bathers pose for the camera, this time on Meadfoot Beach. I believe the date to be about 1910.

(Middle) A queue of fine automobiles (they're far too elegant to be called cars) lined up along the Marine Drive on 15 May 1936. The reason for such a crowd is that the newly built liner *Queen Mary* was cruising along the coast.

(Bottom) Anstey's Cove in the high Edwardian era was a regular destination for excursions from central Torquay; genteel ladies could imagine themselves far from the madding crowd, yet still have a comforting cup of tea.

In this wintry scene of Babbacombe Beach in 1900, the thatched cottage in the foreground is 'The Glen', once the home of Miss Emma Keyse. She was murdered here in 1884. An employee of hers, John Lee, was convicted of the crime and sentenced to death by hanging. He became famous as 'The Man They Couldn't Hang', as three attempts were made to carry out the sentence, but the trapdoors beneath the scaffold refused to open each time. His sentence was commuted to life imprisonment, and he was eventually released.

(Below) It is the summer of 1911, and a row of those weird and wonderful contraptions, bathing machines, are drawn up on Oddicombe Beach. There is no cliff railway at the time, as that wasn't built until 1926, so everyone had to walk down to the beach. Not that walking down the steep hill was ever a problem – it was getting back up it again!

(Opposite) The top picture shows the junction of Teignmouth and Westhill Roads in the 1890s. The houses along Teignmouth Road and one side of Westhill were not built until the 1920s. The sloping fields in the centre of the photograph are now the site of Cuthbert Mayne School. The next view shows St Marychurch; the elegant architecture of the Hampton Court Hotel can be seen. Sadly, the building was demolished to make way for a supermarket. The bottom view is of Maidencombe in the early 20th century. The thatched cottage in the foreground was demolished long ago, but the building in the centre still stands, known today as 'Little Thatch'.

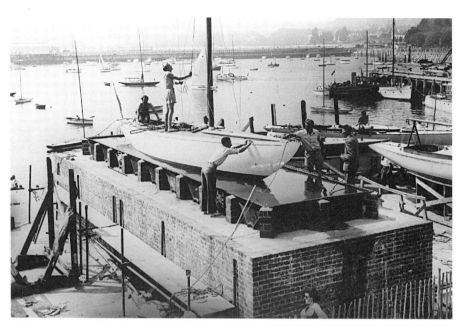

Torquay and Torbay burst onto the international stage in 1948 when the sailing events of that year's Olympic Games were held here. Apparently all yachts entered in the Olympic races had to be measured to ensure that they matched the regulations, and also weighed! This strange-looking contraption, sited on Beacon Quay, did the job; we see a yacht getting the once over.

The opening and closing ceremonies were held on the lawn in front of Torre Abbey, the Olympic Flame burning on a balcony above the Abbey's front door throughout the event. This view of the closing ceremony shows laurel wreaths attached to the competing national flags.

Torquay of Yesteryear

Above, the tram tracks are being laid at the Teignmouth Road junction. The first tram ran here in April 1907.

When the railway line was extended from Torquay to Paignton in the 1860s, it was laid as single track, with a tunnel at Hollicombe, locally known as 'Gasworks Tunnel'. When the company wanted to double the line, it was decided that it would be cheaper to demolish the tunnel and replace it with a cutting. This view shows the tunnel partly removed, with the remains of the northern tunnel mouth in the lower left corner.

With the demolition of the tunnel came the chance to realign the Torquay to Paignton road by building a bridge over the cutting. This view shows the new bridge nearing completion; on the left is the new approach to Wheatridge Lane. The railway tracks seen in the photograph were used by the building contractor.

Finally, it is late afternoon at Torre Station in August 1936; a train hauled by a Bulldog class locomotive is leaving, probably on a Kingswear to Exeter service. Coupled to the front of the train and running tender first is a Castle class engine that will have hauled an express down to Kingswear and is now returning to Newton Abbot for stabling overnight. Hitching it to the front of another train saved having to clear a route just for the engine. The carriage is interesting as it was one of a batch built as ambulance carriages during the First World War, converted for general passenger use only in 1924.

(Back cover) Several generations of the Thomas family ran the catering and boating concessions at Anstey's Cove. This view shows the sign over the door, in Latin, which lists most of the things they were able to supply, including fresh fish, bathing machines and swimming lessons, as well as cream teas.